Start Surfing

Rick Abbott

Start Surfing

Illustrations by Mike Baker

Stanley Paul
London Melbourne Sydney Auckland Johannesburg

Stanley Paul & Co. Ltd

An imprint of the Hutchinson Publishing Group

3 Fitzroy Square, London W1P 6JD

Hutchinson Group (Australia) Pty Ltd
30–32 Cremorne Street, Richmond South, Victoria 3121
PO Box 151, Broadway, New South Wales 2007

Hutchinson Group (NZ) Ltd
32–34 View Road, PO Box 40–086, Glenfield, Auckland 10

Hutchinson Group (SA) (Pty) Ltd
PO Box 337, Bergvlei 2012, South Africa

First published 1980

Typeset by Computacomp (UK) Ltd, Fort William, Scotland

Printed in Great Britain by The Anchor Press Ltd
and bound by Wm Brendon & Son Ltd
both of Tiptree, Essex

ISBN 0 09 140630 7 cased
0 09 140631 5 paper

Acknowledgements

We would like to thank Art Brewer of *Surfer* magazine in California, and Bruce Channon and Hugh McLeod of *Surfing World* magazine in Australia for their help with photographic material. Thanks also to Guy Motil, Joaquin, Woody Woodworth, *Island Style* and Steve Wilkings.

Contents

Introduction

There is no way in the world that somebody will learn to surf just by reading a book about it. Apart from watching other people surf and talking to surfers yourself, the most important thing is to get out in the waves with a board and give it a try. In spite of the fact that surfing may look uncomplicated however, there is really quite a lot to learn. The broad aim of this book is to give beginners or relative newcomers easy access to the information that should be the most useful to them. If it makes the learning process quicker, sheds light on some of the mysteries and mystiques and helps to save money and avoid mistakes when purchasing boards and wetsuits, then its role will have been fulfilled.

The chapters have been arranged so as not to bombard the absolute beginner with too many complications early in the book. After an introduction to the surfboard and wetsuits and the various other bits and pieces we use, the first practical section discusses only enough to be able to catch and stand up on a wave, turn the way you want to go and leave the wave with some semblance of control. By definition, I suppose, when you can do that you're a surfer; but there remains plenty of scope! Chapters four and five are about where surfing waves come from (plenty of experienced surfers are pretty clueless about this), and the various types of surfing 'break'. The next two sections return to practical surfing and board design. These are intended for people who already have some surfing experience.

In order that the book shouldn't be too overladen with tales of caution and woe, and boring lists of do's and don'ts, I have summarised all the 'nasties' in the last chapter. If you have surfed only a little or not at all, you should definitely read chapter eight in addition to the early part of the book.

Over the last fifteen years or so, board surfing has become more and more popular and in western countries with an ocean seaboard it is now a major sport. In areas like California and parts of Australia which

Burleigh, Queensland (Surfing World)

have large centres of population near the surf, conditions are often so crowded that surfers are willing to drive long distances to find quieter waves. Surfing has spread to less 'developed' parts of the world as well and is now practised to a surprisingly high standard in a whole range of unspoilt locations. Although surfboard materials come from the petrochemical industries, the outlay on equipment is much less than for many other forms of water sport.

Ever since the 1950s there has been a popularised 'image' of surfing and surfers. This 'surfing cult' originated in the USA and has been exploited ever since by commercial interests. Although it is true that, as with any absorbing art form or sport, certain participants become fanatical and arrange their lives around the activity, it is also true that surfing is not the sole domain of a bunch of anarchists who communicate in 'surfing language' and listen to nothing but 'surfing music'. Surfing is practised by an extremely wide range of people whose aims and aspirations vary accordingly. It would, of course, be extremely narrow-minded to believe that one's own approach was the ultimate.

Organised surfing competitions are not covered in this book. Competitions involve a small number of surfers and lots of onlookers and I am only concerned here with people who actually want to participate rather than treat surfing as a spectator sport. In the last few years a group of the world's top surfers have created a 'professional' competition circuit which takes in events in Hawaii, the USA, Australia, South Africa and Brazil. These events are sponsored to various degrees and the top performers obtain money prizes. At present however, the amount of interest shown by the commercial sponsors is so low (certainly when compared with golf or tennis), that only the top three or four superstars could possibly hope to make a year long living from the prize money. Apparently, whether these competitions prove to be good television material has a lot to do with the overall success of the venture. In the meantime they give the magazines plenty of good pictures and material to get their teeth into and they undoubtedly raise overall surfing standards. Naturally enough there is a certain amount of opposition to this professional circuit idea, not least from the local surfers whose favourite break is commandeered during one of the rare periods of good surf in the year.

Organisers of professional contests realised very quickly that for the surf to be good enough to justify holding a competition in the first place, not only did you have to choose a top location in the best season but you had to have a 'waiting period' of one or two weeks for something sufficiently worthwhile to happen in the wave department. Even then, the surf can be notoriously uncooperative and the competition that eventually goes ahead out of sheer desperation simply proves who is the best 'magician' in miniature slop! If you transfer these same problems to the various amateur competitions that take place, when people have neither the money nor the inclination to indulge in waiting periods, you arrive at the ludicrous spectacle of an event being firmly scheduled for a one or two day period. When the chances of even reasonable surf are about one in ten, it is hardly surprising that the bulk of competitions are plagued by postponements or poor waves.

Many of the enthusiasts of other sports (dinghy sailing for instance) claim that organised competition is necessary to sustain a high level of interest and participation over many years. Surfing isn't like that, partly because the degree of challenge and fascination remains fairly high in any case but also because, in a completely non-organised manner, it is inherently fiercely competitive. This applies not only to wave-catching ploys in crowds but also to everybody trying to out-perform one another. As in any art form where performance cannot be assessed in terms of speed or distance, and where any kind of judgement is highly subjective in any case, perhaps the best analysis is the kind arrived at by the silent observations of those paddling back out.

I haven't made any specific reference to women in this book. Girls do of course surf, and some of them surf at a very high standard. Far fewer girls become involved in surfing than boys – for reasons I won't even attempt to go into. Every scrap of information in the book is intended for people of either sex, and it is no easier or more difficult for females to learn to surf than males.

Many other forms of surfing, a couple of which are mentioned in passing in the book, exist alongside standup or kneeboard surfing. Each has its devotees and particular merits. By not discussing them I do not intend to imply that they are inferior in any way to the type of surfing I have chosen for myself and therefore feel most qualified to write about. They include, in no particular order, the use of slalom or surf kayaks, surf skis, surf catamarans, sailboards (windsurfers), dories, surf boats, airmats, paipo-boards, belly-boards and bodysurfing.

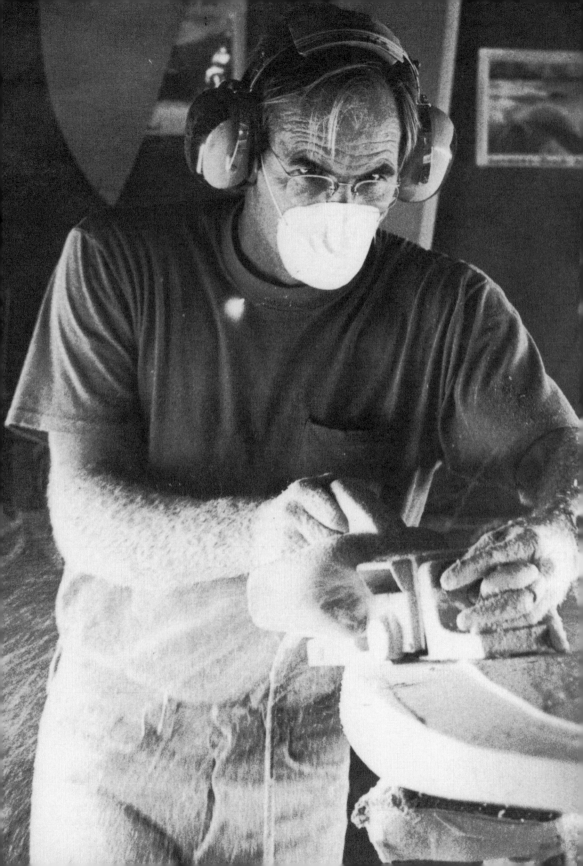

Chapter One
The Board

History

The long and interesting history of surfboard design and construction merits a book of its own. The following is a brief summary of the major turning points in the development of today's board and a mention of the handful of individuals who are generally credited with the introduction of the most significant advances.

Riding waves with a board can hardly be considered a new art. Some authorities believe that the natives of the Hawaiian Islands were using surfboards a thousand years ago. Certainly, when Christian missionaries arrived there in the nineteenth century, surfing had been a major pastime for centuries. A typical board at that time was about 6ft long, 16in wide and about a foot thick. Many were constructed of a very light wood called wiliwili, which is similar to balsa. The missionaries attempted to prohibit surfing and the sport declined. By the time surfing was reborn in Hawaii, after the period of missionary domination, the most popular boards were big and very heavy.

Duke Kahanamoku, an Olympic swimming champion from Hawaii, was instrumental in the spread of board surfing to California and Australia in the early 1900s, his first visit to Australia being in 1915. His travels and expert demonstrations triggered the formation of small surf groups in these two areas which, along with Hawaii, were to develop into the surfing strongholds of the world. 'The Duke' was very powerfully built and carrying his solid and heavy boards probably didn't present him with too many problems.

Even in the 1930s, surfing was still very much a minor sport. By then however, there were surfers with sufficient enthusiasm and inventiveness to try out new ideas and materials. The most important of these individuals was Tom Blake, who in observing the underwater appendages of racing powerboats realised that the addition of a 'skeg' to the bottom of a surfboard near the tail might give the board much needed directional stability and stop it 'spinning out'. In

Californian Shaper, Mike Eaton at work (Guy Motil)

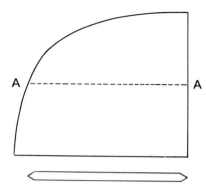

Longboard skeg, with cross section indicated

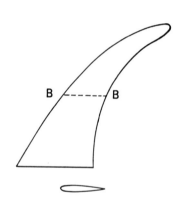

Greenough fin, with cross section indicated

1935 he tried this with a modified skeg salvaged from a wrecked powerboat and found it to be a great success, although according to Blake it took another ten years for skegs to be widely adopted. While modern 'fins' are more functional in plan and cross-section, the original type of skeg (left) was used until the late 1960s.

Tom Blake also introduced hollow wooden boards which became widely adopted at that time. These were much lighter than the previously used 80-pound redwood solids, and led the way to the re-introduction of balsa.

The Second World War encouraged advances in new construction materials. One such development was the combination of glass filaments and plastic resin known as glassfibre. The first surfer to cover surfboards with glassfibre successfully was a Californian called Bob Simmons, who used it first on balsa and then on plywood. Glassfibre has never been improved on as a covering for boards. Simmons was also responsible for several new design ideas such as modifications to plan shape and bottom shape that have had a lasting influence.

Another new material introduced which has not been bettered was expanded polyurethane foam, utilised as a surfboard core material. After various adventures and several laboratory explosions in the mid-50s, two more Californians, Gordon Clark and Hobie Alter, successfully arrived at the correct formulae and methods to enable them to produce moulded surfboard 'blanks' from polyurethane foam. Clark now heads one of the biggest board blank concerns in the world and Alter is best known for his range of fast and highly successful 'Hobie Cat' catamarans.

When I started surfing in Durban in 1966, the average board length was 9ft 9in. Boards throughout the surfing world at that time were very similar. Rails were rounded and were almost parallel to each other; tails were square, bottoms were dome-shaped in cross section, the wide point was behind centre and there was lots of tail lift (plan shape opposite).

At about that time, a surfer living in California called George Greenough started to design an entirely new surfboard fin and was riding his own kneeboards in an apparently amazing manner. Greenough's fins and ideas on board design were to have a lasting effect on future developments but it wasn't until he took his new equipment to Australia that his theories were adopted by others. His fins, which were based on those of high-speed fish, were narrow, raked back, and perhaps most importantly of all, 'foiled'.

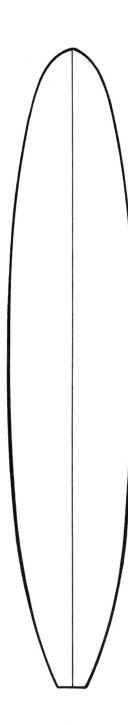

By 1967 Greenough's kneeboards, which were short, wide and highly manoeuvrable, had begun to have an effect on the design of standup surfboards in Australia. Bob McTavish and others were building and riding boards that bore little resemblance to anything that had come before. These Australian surfboards were short (about 8ft long), wide (up to 25in), had fairly parallel rails and wide tails and had a very pronounced V bottom for as much as the rear half of the board's length. In the same year, McTavish along with Nat Young and Ted Spencer took their lightweight Vs to Hawaii and although the boards were ultra-snappy in small waves, they were found to be too wide and slow for the more powerful waves of the north shore spots.

By this time, much smaller boards were being experimented with by Hawaiian residents too. Largely as a result of the need for speed, shapers such as Dick Brewer were building sleek, pointed boards called 'mini-guns'. Although some of these boards were extremely narrow (as little as 16in), the planshape of a modern, big wave board is almost the same.

The validity of shorter, lighter equipment was being accepted by growing numbers of surfers by 1968, leading to what has been termed by the surfing media 'The Shortboard Revolution'. Previously accepted designs and styles were abandoned everywhere. Anyone who fancied their chances as a shaper got busy buying second grade blanks and borrowing electric planers in their search for extra speed and manoeuvrability. Everything in the design field was attempted, with shortness being the only common factor. Inevitably, many went to rather optimistic extremes.

The late 60s and 70s have seen rapid growth in the numbers of people surfing and consequently many more surfers have become involved in the board-building industry. Subtle but important changes in board design have occurred throughout this period resulting in todays' aesthetically pleasing and functional shapes. The nature of the waves to be ridden will always have a very strong influence on design features. There is no such thing as a board that will ride 2ft and 10ft waves equally well.

Parts of a board

In spite of the fact that the design variations of surfboards are limitless, the named parts of a board are few and simple.

The top surface on which you lie and stand is called the deck and what used to be called the skeg is now the fin (sometimes there are two). Any allusion to things nautical end here because the bow is called the nose, the stern is called the tail and the gunwales, or edges, are called rails! A strong leash attachment on the board's deck is also a desirable feature.

Main board types and their construction
Modern surfboards can be divided into three main types depending on the way they are constructed or the amount of finish they are given.

Moulded or 'pop-out' boards
These boards are the least expensive and their construction has much in common with that of glassfibre boats. The deck and bottom are each 'laid up' in separate moulds. These two halves are then joined around the rails after a brown foam mixture has been poured into the bottom half. Each pop-out made from the same mould is exactly the same shape and this shape relies entirely on the characteristics of the original plug used for that mould's construction.

Pop-outs are heavier than more expensive boards but because they are aimed at the holiday and novice market, they make excellent boards for beginners. By modern standards their dimensions are fairly generous and they therefore possess adequate buoyancy and stability. Because there is a ready market for used pop-outs, the resale value of such a board in reasonable condition remains relatively high.

Exploded section through a moulded or pop-out surfboard

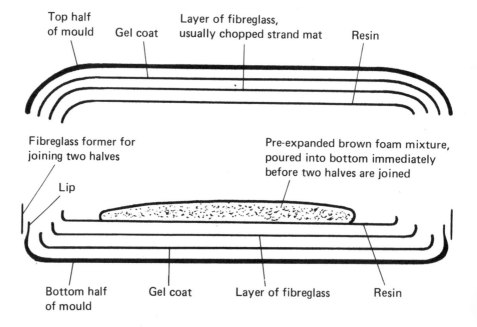

Top half of mould   Gel coat   Layer of fibreglass, usually chopped strand mat   Resin

Fibreglass former for joining two halves

Lip

Pre-expanded brown foam mixture, poured into bottom immediately before two halves are joined

Bottom half of mould   Gel coat   Layer of fibreglass   Resin

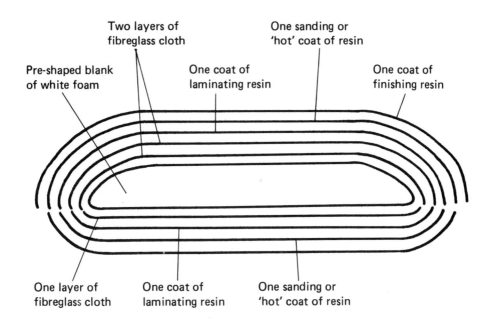

Two layers of fibreglass cloth

One sanding or 'hot' coat of resin

Pre-shaped blank of white foam

One coat of laminating resin

One coat of finishing resin

One layer of fibreglass cloth

One coat of laminating resin

One sanding or 'hot' coat of resin

Exploded section through a custom surfboard

Custom boards

These boards are made in a different manner from pop-outs and are lighter, more expensive and usually more sophisticated. Carefully measured and mixed foam components are poured in liquid form into a steel and concrete mould that is the shape and size of a fat board. The foam components react together very quickly to fill the inside of the mould forming a light but tough, white polyurethane foam blank. Each blank is shaped by hand until it is the exact dimensions of the required board. The blank is then laminated with polyester resin and glass cloth (usually two layers of cloth on the deck and one on the bottom) and the fin is attached. A filler coat (or hot coat) of resin is applied to each side. The board is then sanded all over, a gloss coat of thinned resin applied to both sides and finally the board is rubbed down with wet carborundum paper and then polished.

The characteristics and quality of a shaped blank depend upon the size and shape of the original blank and the skill and experience of the guy doing the shaping. Custom construction allows for a vast range of board types which give great scope for experimentation. The custom board process allows an experienced surfer to obtain a board with very specific design features. Consequently most custom type boards are fairly slender, are pretty highly tuned and are generally not suitable for beginners – even old battered ones that are fairly cheap.

Hot-coat custom boards

The cost of a custom-type board can be reduced considerably by leaving out the last four manufacturing processes. In other words, such boards are sold unsanded after the application of the filler or hot coats of resin. In this way a lot of time is saved and such a board will be quite strong enough and give excellent service after some careful rubbing down by the customer. Although a gloss coat adds slightly to the strength of a board, its main function is to enhance the board's appearance.

The chief disadvantage of hot-coat models is that because they are a cheaper version of full custom boards, less care is taken in their shaping. On the other hand, such boards held in stock are usually aimed at the beginners' market and, like pop-outs, they have good flotation and stability and consequently make excellent boards for novices.

Plan shape and size

The usual way to describe a surfboard is to give the dimensions and general characteristics of its planshape. Many more details can be added to these of course and are discussed more fully in chapter 7.

The dimensions used are first, the overall length, followed by three figures consisting of: the width 1ft from the nose, the maximum width and the width 1ft from the tail. The dimensions of the board on the left for instance are: 7ft, $14\frac{1}{2}$in–21in–$13\frac{1}{2}$in.

The widest point of most boards lies 3–6in in front of centre. The width 1ft from the nose is usually between 1 and 2in greater than the width 1ft from the tail. (The difference in the case of 'Stingers' is usually between 2 and $3\frac{1}{2}$in. See chapter 7.) The vast majority of contemporary boards are between 6ft and 7ft 6in long and the average maximum width is around 20in. Eighteen and a half inches width would be considered very narrow and 22in would be considered wide.

The planshape of a board's tail is an important part of that board's general description. Tail shapes are fairly varied, very easy to assess and their importance as a design feature is usually over-emphasised when compared with rocker (see below) thickness distribution, rail shape, fin design and position and so on.

Rocker

Rocker is the name given to the longitudinal curvature of the bottom of the board. The nature of the rocker is probably the most important design feature of any surfboard.

In fairly simple terms, rocker starts at the front with

pronounced 'nose lift', then gets flatter (but not dead flat), for efficient planing and then curves upwards behind the fin – 'tail lift'. If a straight edge is held against the mid-point of a good modern board, the distance from the straight edge to the nose will be 3–5in and the distance to the tail will be somewhere between $1^1/_2$ and $2^1/_2$in.

Page 19 shows a typical modern full-length rocker. The nose rocker of the 7ft board in the illustration is $4^1/_2$in and the tail rocker is $1^1/_2$in.

Thickness distribution

When viewed from the edge, the deck and bottom of a board should display smooth, flowing lines with no abrupt changes in direction or bumps. The thickest portion of a board should coincide with the widest section. See below for contemporary thickness distribution. The exact thickness and total volume of any board will of course depend on the required amount of buoyancy.

Boards for beginners

Several major factors are going to affect the success or otherwise of your surfing: your own natural ability and fitness, the abundance and quality of rideable waves in your area, the size of the crowd you may have to compete against for waves, the amount of time you spend in the water and finally, the design of your board.

The crowd problem, if it exists at all, is sometimes avoided by spending longer on the road. Surfing is sufficiently difficult to prevent those with a half-hearted approach from having much success. This is a good thing in my opinion – it was never my intention to sell the sport. You will only become a surfer if you possess a high degree of motivation.

It is very difficult to learn to surf with a board that is not suitable. I've already generally described the types of board that might be OK – now for specifics.

Because of increased media coverage and the colourful image that goes with surfing, it is easier than ever to end up buying a board that looks great on the roofrack or under your arm but isn't so great on a wave. Spray jobs, sunsets and pin lines are all very nice but they don't make a scrap of difference when it comes to taking that final stroke and scrambling to your feet.

Typical rocker and thickness distribution of a modern board

If you are a beginner or novice who wants to progress fairly quickly on modern equipment, you should be looking for a board with a smooth, contemporary type of plan shape, a proven distribution of thickness, plus the following:

(a) Sufficient width, especially in the middle and tail, to provide easy planing on small waves.

(b) Sufficient thickness and therefore buoyancy to produce easy paddling and fairly easy wave-catching.

(c) Full length, gradual rocker.

(d) Low rails that are very soft in the nose and middle, getting harder towards the tail.

(e) Correctly foiled fin (with rounded leading edge and no sharp edges or point), set fairly well back.

(f) Strong leash attachment on the deck.

As I have already mentioned, modern, good quality pop-outs often make good beginners' boards. They may be *too* buoyant for people weighing about 112lb and under, however. Too much flotation is as undesirable in a learner's board as too little because it will make the board too 'corky' and difficult to control.

If you are in a position to choose either a hot-coat or full custom board from a large stock or intend having a board specially made, your weight should determine the board's dimensions. Page 18 shows the plan shape of a board I would recommend to someone weighing around 140lb. The board shown has a round tail, is 7ft long with widths of 14^1/$_2$in–21in–13^1/$_2$in. The maximum thickness should be at least 3in. As long as the other design features are as listed above then such a board should be suitable for progression well beyond the learning stage.

For learners weighing more or less than 140lb I would simply recommend a scaled up or scaled down version of the board already outlined. Typical dimensions would be as follows. For someone weighing about 100lb: 6ft 6in long, about 20in maximum width and about 2^1/$_2$in maximum thickness. For someone weighing approximately 180lb: 7ft 6in long, between 21 and 21^1/$_2$in wide and between 3^1/$_4$in and 3^1/$_2$in maximum thickness.

Board care

If you want your board to retain its value and good looks, treat it with loving care. A well cared for board will go better too.

Strong sunlight ages resin and makes it brittle; it also fades colours and turns clear boards brown. Whilst this hazard is conspicuous by its absence about eighty per cent of the time in the gloomy weather belts, such as

Britain, keep your board out of bright sun whenever possible. Store it in a cool, shaded place at home and keep it in a stout board-bag when on the move.

With even the most indulgent protection, your board is going to get damaged whilst in use. If the damage is minor then cover the spot with waterproof tape until you can make a permanent repair. If the damage is more serious and exposes rough edges of fibreglass, it is best to leave the water immediately to avoid entry of salt water into the board and avoid personal injury.

Take the trouble to find out how to repair your board properly, or have it done professionally. Always rub down repairs flush with the surrounding surface. Metal polish makes a good substitute for polishing compound.

Never store a board flat or with heavy objects resting on top whilst it is supported only at each end because it will change shape. A friend of mine travelled to Biarritz with his board upside down on the roof rack and a suitcase strapped on top. He arrived with a board with no rocker!

The easiest way to write a board off (and perhaps kill somebody else in the process), is to have it part company with the roof rack whilst travelling at speed. Always pad roof racks with some type of foam but above all make sure the roof rack is fixed securely to the roof and the board is secured to the rack properly. Soft, man-made cord is much safer than elastic.

Chapter Two
Equipment

Wetsuits

In all but the very warmest of climates, surfers wear various types of garment made from closed-cell rubber known as neoprene. In tropical areas vests or 'shorties' are often adequate covering and their design is relatively unimportant. As water and air temperatures get lower, wetsuits become more complicated and expensive and their design becomes much more important.

The best type of wetsuit for surfing in Britain (and areas with a similar climate), is undoubtedly a one piece garment with long arms and long legs. Only in midsummer is it possible to be comfortable for several hours with less rubber. Since the best surfing does not occur in midsummer, I will concentrate on the one-piece suit. First though, let's look at why wetsuits should keep us warm at all.

A dry wetsuit is warmer than a wet one! They keep us warm in spite of being wet inside and not because of it. Consequently, cold water suits should inhibit the entry of cold water. Neoprene, because of its closed-cell structure, is a very efficient insulator and therefore much of the heat generated by your body is retained inside.

Wetsuit rubber is lined on the inside with a thin layer of very flexible nylon. This lining makes the suit much easier to put on and take off and it also makes the garment much stronger. Neoprene with a layer of nylon on the inside only is usually called 'single-lined'. 'Double-lined' neoprene, which has a layer of nylon on each side of the rubber, is also available and there are various pros and cons for its use. While more expensive than single-lined neoprene it is much stronger, and not only is it more resistant to snagging and abrasion but the material next to the seams stays intact much longer. Due to the slightly increased evaporation in a strong breeze, double-lined neoprene is not quite as warm as single-lined (although the difference appears to be quite small). Nylon on the outside also allows the introduction of colour to the garment. On balance, therefore, it is almost certainly worth paying the extra for double-lined

Wipeout with leash (Surfing World)

material since the suit will last longer. Quite a good compromise is a suit with double-lined body and legs, and single-lined arms and shoulders.

The usual thickness for a cool-water wetsuit is 3mm. Warm water suits are often 2mm thick and suits for very cold conditions can be as thick as 6mm.

Wetsuit seams are usually glued and then stitched. If a suit is to be as warm as possible, it is essential that the seams are watertight. This is usually achieved by using a sewing machine that produces a blind stitch – the seams are sewn on the nylon side while the needle does not pass right through the rubber. When used in conjunction with modern binary glues, such seams are surprisingly strong. Further reinforcement is sometimes provided by the application, using heat, of nylon tape over the stitching. If maximum warmth is not so important, then seams are either glued and sewn with a conventional zigzag stitch or glued and reinforced with elasticated nylon tape applied with a four needle German 'Mauser' machine. Both types of seam let in water. The Mauser technique is especially strong but it does leak a lot due to the large number of stitch holes.

The type of wetsuit I am now manufacturing for hardcore surfers in cooler conditions is as follows. The body and legs are in 4 mm double-lined material and the arms, which are continuous from wrist to wrist across the shoulders are double-lined. If single-lined material is used, then the knee, crutch and underarm areas should be made from double-lined rubber to prevent wear. All the seams are blind stitched (and these should be glued with binary adhesive). The collar is high and is fully adjustable with the use of Velcro fastening. The body zip is placed to one side of the chest. There are no wrist or ankle zips, since these simply let in more water. Finally, because the body and legs consist of two pieces only, seams are minimal.

From May to October, the only conditions under which a lesser coverage of neoprene is really comfortable are firstly, the rare occasions when there is surf, sun and little wind and secondly, if you are naturally endowed with your own supply of bodily insulation.

In more northern latitudes things start to get a bit cool in November. For the next five months it can at times get very cold. With the right equipment and sufficient enthusiasm however, it is possible to surf right through the winter without too much discomfort. (At the time of writing, February, we are having to walk through snow on the beach to get to our waves). When it starts to get really cold it is desirable to wear a thicker layer of neoprene and to cover head, hands and feet. The cheapest way to increase the thickness of neoprene is to wear either a 2mm vest or a shortie under your existing suit. An advantage of this method is that the cold water that inevitably leaks through the zip has to travel further before it gets to your skin. The obvious alternative is to have a special winter suit made from thicker rubber.

Blind stitched socks with long ankles are the warmest type of footwear, but hard-soled neoprene boots last longer, and are most suitable if your surfing involves long walks over concrete, pebbles or rocks. Blind stitched mittens with long wrists keep the hands warm even in mid winter, and a very popular head warmer in this part of the world is a neoprene version of a water polo cap with a fairly tight neoprene chin strap. Many surfers find that traditional wetsuit hoods limit head movement too much and impede hearing and therefore balance. Some form of head cover is essential, however, since heat loss via the head is considerable.

Wetsuit care
Wetsuits, like surfboards, will last longer if treated carefully. After use they should be rinsed in cool, fresh water and hung up inside out to drip dry. They should be stored in a cool place, out of direct sunlight and kept on a padded hanger. If they are left folded or stored with sharp objects on top, the neoprene will become permanently damaged.

Blind stitching sometimes comes undone in short sections and can be hand sewn with a small needle and Terylene thread, avoiding pushing the needle right through the material. Wetsuit manufacturers are able to provide off-cuts of neoprene and suitable glue for you to repair tears and abrasion. Major repairs and the fitting of new zips are probably best done professionally.

Left. *Machine made 'blind stitch'*

Right. *Hand sewn equivalent of 'blind stitch'*

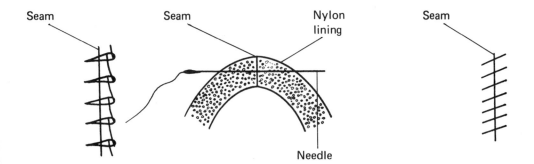

Seam   Seam   Nylon lining   Seam

Needle

Leashes

The introduction of the leash in the late 1960s has had a marked effect on surfing. Leashes are now used by practically all surfers in all but the largest of waves.

A good quality modern leash consists of about 5ft of tubular rubber inside which is a length of coiled nylon line. One end of the line is attached to a 'leash cup' or fibreglass loop at the rear of the board's deck, while the other end is attached to the surfer's ankle by means of a nylon webbing loop fitted with Velcro. When you fall off your board, the rubber tubing absorbs the initial shock and the nylon line acts as a stretch limiter. The chief advantages of a leash are:

(a) Much less time is taken up in retrieving boards after wipeouts. This is particularly useful for beginners.

(b) Surf locations with hostile, rocky shorelines can be, and are, much more widely ridden.

The possible disadvantages of the leash are:

(a) With much fewer people having to swim to the beach for their board, a crowded takeoff area stays crowded.

(b) Many surfers who have taken up surfing since the beginning of the leash era have little experience of *surf swimming*. This is a potentially dangerous lack of experience (also see chapter eight).

(c) Surfers sometimes get struck in the face or eyes by the tail of a board springing back after a wipeout. Eyes have been lost this way. Beware of sharp 'pintails' and 'swallowtails' when used in conjunction with very stretchy leashes (i.e. those with very thin nylon line).

(d) It is impossible to get far away from the board in heavier-than-usual wipeouts. This can, at times, be worrying.

In powerful waves, a leash may cut right into the tail rail after a wipeout. A length (about 1 ft) of broad nylon tape connecting the leash to the normal point of attachment on the board will greatly minimise this risk. Such lengths of tape are available commercially and are usually called 'rail savers'.

Wax

Special wax is manufactured for application to surfboard decks and frequent application of such wax will stop bare feet or wetsuit boots from slipping on the wet glassfibre. Wax is also soft and therefore kind to skin and neoprene. Board wax is produced in different hardnesses for different climates; soft for cold and hard for hot. Bare skin tropical surfers should avoid the possibility of infection to small cuts and grazes on chest and stomach by removing dirty wax fairly frequently. To wax the deck of a new board, start with fairly light circular rubbing and then increase pressure after the initial thin build up. With subsequent applications of wax, the build-up will gradually get quite thick and lumpy. Wetsuited surfers needn't worry about this rather dirty-looking accumulation, although those with ultra-light boards may object to all this extra weight they will be pushing around!

If a damaged board deck has to be repaired, it is essential to remove every scrap of wax from the area to be worked on, otherwise the new resin will not bond properly to the board. The quickest way to do this is to use the sharp edge of a square-sectioned piece of wood followed by sanding with several small pieces of fairly coarse glass paper or carborundum paper. Foam dust from a shaping-room floor is also very efficient if rubbed on the area to be cleaned. Hot water will also take most of the wax off very quickly but it has a tendency to transfer a thin coating of wax onto the bottom of the board where it is definitely not required.

Chapter Three
Early Skills

Definition of wave size

The average surfer probably spends ninety per cent of his time riding surf under five feet.

BILL HAMILTON. *Surfer Magazine.*

Any surfer's definition of wave size depends on his attitude and where he's used to surfing. Consequently, a description such as 'medium-size' can cover a wide range. The height of a wave for surfing is the vertical measurement from the trough to the crest just before the wave breaks. This height is always estimated of course.

It is necessary, I feel, to set down a definition of sizes. With Hamilton's statement very much in mind, my definition encompasses the average conditions a surfer will encounter in most of the world's surfing grounds. Waves of twenty feet and over are ridden each winter on the northern shores of the Hawaiian Islands but for most of us, the surfing masses, such spectacles will be seen only in magazines or on the silver screen.

SMALL	1ft–4ft
MEDIUM	4ft–6ft
BIG	6ft–10ft
VERY BIG	10ft and over

Walking out

When entering surf from a gently shelving beach it is usual to wade into waist-deep water before diving onto the board and commencing to paddle. If you make the mistake of holding the board *across* the front of your body whilst walking out, the advancing lines of whitewater ('soup') will very quickly slam the board into your face! To avoid this, hold the board beside you with the nose pointing at the oncoming waves.

If the lines of soup are fairly powerful and you have reached the point where you want to start paddling into deeper water, it is often a good idea to wait for a lull. If you place one hand on the tail of the board and the other hand about half way along the deck you can make the nose of the board ride up and over the broken waves while you wait.

Rudy White surfing in Florida (Joaquin)

Paddling

'Longboards' can be paddled in a prone or a kneeling position; 'shortboards' can only be paddled in a prone position. To operate in water more than waist deep and to catch unbroken waves, you will need to become fairly proficient at prone paddling.

A shortboard can only be paddled efficiently if you lie in exactly the right place. Many beginners make the mistake of lying too near the tail causing the nose to stick up in the air. A board 'trimmed' as badly as this is very inefficient and paddling such a vessel is a quick route to total exhaustion.

This page shows a shortboard being prone-paddled in the correct manner. Only the leading few inches of the board's bottom should be clear of the surface. Extra stability can be provided by spreading your legs slightly and trailing a foot in the water each side of the board. (This also creates extra drag of course.)

Catching soup

Before venturing into deep water for the first time, it is a good idea to spend some time catching and riding the lines of soup on the shoreward side of the area where the waves are breaking. This will give you a fair idea of how your board moves through the water without the complications (and frustrations) of catching unbroken ('green') waves.

To catch a wave that has already broken, you will need to propel the board forwards at the correct moment. In thigh-deep water you can launch and dive onto the board *just* before the soup reaches you (as with a belly-board), and in water deeper than this you will need to prone-paddle the board to get up plenty of speed *before* the wave reaches you.

As well as riding soup in a prone position, it is a good time to practise standing up. Remember however, that because the whitewater from small waves doesn't push a board forward very fast, the board will be less stable than when it is sliding across the face of a green wave. (When you go into deeper water and progress to the

Prone paddling

30

'real thing', this extra stability will probably seem like the only bit of good news around for some time.)

Remember to get off the board before testing the fin to destruction in the shallows.

Standing up and stance

Progress in learning to surf will be much quicker if you make an effort to get to your feet on a board in the correct manner. By this I mean that you should transfer from a lying to a standing position swiftly and in one movement *without* kneeling in between. A common mistake amongst novices is to spend too much time riding the soup in a kneeling position. They eventually find it very hard to stand up in one go.

Standing up efficiently and quickly involves a fairly explosive and athletic movement. It is definitely worthwhile practising this skill on dry land. You should endeavour to place your feet in the positions that will give you maximum stability and will trim the board effectively *before* your hands leave the deck. This will minimise any unstable shuffling of feet. You will quite naturally adopt a stance either with the left foot forward – 'natural foot' – or with the right foot forward – 'goofy-foot'. The distance you place your feet apart and the precise position for correct trim of your particular board will be discovered by trial and error. Never stand too erect with stiff legs. Flexed, rubbery legs provide a lower centre of gravity and therefore better stability as well as absorbing the impact of bumpy wave-faces.

Paddling out

The majority of surfing situations require fairly frequent bouts of paddling out through soup. In fairly heavy surf this can be very strenuous and requires a high degree of skill to be accomplished with a minimum of energy loss. Where there is deep water access to the break, paddling out can be relatively hassle-free but when the surf is breaking against a fairly ordinary strip of sandy coastline, the prospect of battling through line after line of surging whitewater can be formidable.

Careful observation of your intended field of operation is always worthwhile. If the surf is big enough to cause problems, there will nearly always be slightly deeper channels carrying water from the breaking waves seawards. This type of water flow is called a 'rip'. Use rips to paddle out in whenever possible. Good surfing waves arrive in groups called 'sets'. Between each set there is a lull. By observation and careful timing, the longer lulls can be productively utilised for getting 'outside'.

These pages show the most popular techniques for getting through or over whitewater with a board used in conjunction with a leash. The illustrations are arranged roughly in ascending order of surf size, the 'push-up' at the smaller end of the scale and the 'throw-away' at the bigger end!

Each surfer develops his own group of techniques and the decision to use a particular method at any one time quickly becomes subconscious and fairly spontaneous. Any list such as this is bound to be rather subjective but although other methods exist, the following will at least give you something to work at.

1. PUSH-UP
    Adequate in very small waves. The bulk of the whitewater passes between the deck and the surfer's chest.

2. BACK-THROUGH
    This is sometimes a useful method of waiting for a lull without expending too much energy. As long as you sit well back on the board and keep the tail deep, the bottom of the board should create sufficient resistance for you not to lose too much ground.

3. SIT-BACK
    This method consists of two distinct movements. Firstly the surfer sits well back on his board (facing the wave), and rocks well back so that the nose points high in the air. A split second before the soup hits the underside of the board's nose he rocks violently forward while firmly holding the rails. The timing is critical but for heavier surfers in fairly small waves it can be surprisingly effective. When it is successful, the board travels right over the top of the soup.

4. POWER-THROUGH
    Very popular and quite effective as long as the waves aren't too powerful. The great advantage of this method is that when successful, it creates the minimum interruption to normal paddling and forward progress.

5. ARM OVER

When broken waves become too powerful for the previous methods to be much use, it is necessary to use the body as a type of sea-anchor below the area of main turbulence. The quickest way of doing this is to roll sideways off the board at the last minute, grasping the nose area of the board as securely as possible with one arm.

6. ROLL UNDER

A complex but more secure version of arm over. This method used to be very popular in the old days for longboards without leashes.

7. THROW AWAY

In certain situations it is futile to even attempt to keep hold of your board. The best bet then is to acknowledge this fact before the wave arrives. If you push the board away to one side, this should prevent you being tumbled around with (and perhaps colliding with) the board. You can then sink downwards feet first to gain relatively undisturbed water below the area of heaviest whitewater. Whether the board then drags you shorewards by the leash depends on the size of the waves and the way they are breaking. If such dragging becomes excessive it may be time to un-leash or make other plans.

Because surfers lose or throw away their boards in trying situations it is not wise to paddle out immediately behind someone else.

Catching unbroken waves

Your first experience of real surfing will occur when you catch an unbroken wave and stand up. Unless you are an aquatic genius, you must expect this to be more difficult than catching soup. The acceleration will probably surprise you and you will possibly fall off the back of the board the first few times. Try to anticipate this by leaning forward slightly as if jumping onto a patch of ice for a slide, or as if setting off downhill on a skateboard.

A surfboard is able to move very quickly down the face of a green wave because it 'planes'. Planing, in this context, is the term used to describe the way in which various types of lightweight hull are capable of skimming across the *surface* of the water at high speed. A planing hull is supported by 'dynamic lift' rather than by normal buoyancy. High performance sailing dinghies, small powerboats, waterskis and modern surfboards are all designed to plane easily and very efficiently. The powerboat is pushed along by a noisy, fuel-gobbling engine whereas the sailing boat harnesses the natural force of the wind. The planing 'power' for a surfboard is provided by the combined weight of surfer and board being pulled by gravity down the hill of smooth water even though the water itself is moving *upwards*, i.e. from trough to crest.

The best type of wave for acquiring all early skills including this one, is one provided by a small, even swell moving in over a fairly gradually shoaling sandy bottom. The height of the waves just before they break should preferably be around the 2–3ft mark. A very light offshore wind or no wind at all is highly desirable. If the wind is cross-shore or onshore it will need to be very light indeed not to wreck the surf. The shoreline should be sandy and friendly.

More experienced surfers tend to favour a fairly fast, hard-breaking wave. Such waves are best avoided by beginners for two reasons. Firstly, crowded, competitive areas of activity tend to be rather hostile for beginners and secondly, a beginner's wave should be fairly slow to allow maximum time for catching and experimenting.

The amount of time you subsequently spend riding waves will depend to a large extent on the skill you develop at catching them. The wave you choose needs to be steep enough to *allow* the board to plane. Good 'positioning' in relation to where the waves are breaking is most important here. Always start paddling *before* the wave reaches you and be aggressive and determined about it. Longer, more buoyant boards paddle faster and

Standing up just after catching an unbroken wave

boards with wide tails plane earlier and more easily on small waves. Always wait until the board has started to plane before standing up but then do so quickly.

Turning

Once you've caught and stood up on an unbroken wave, the natural thing for the board to do is plane down the face of the wave and then travel ahead of the wave into flat water where it runs out of energy and stalls. To keep the board planing you will need to turn at the bottom of the wave to get back onto the wave face. This very important first turn is called a 'bottom turn'.

A good surfing wave breaks, or 'peels off', in one definite direction along its length. A 'forehand' bottom turn (in the direction you naturally face), is much easier to learn than a 'backhand' one. For these reasons, a natural foot should utilise waves breaking rightwards, ('rights'), and a goofy-foot should use 'lefts'.

A planing surfboard is made to turn by pressing one rail downwards. This causes increased drag on that side and the board will react by travelling in an arc. To set up this increased drag along one rail all you have to do is transfer some of your weight in that direction, i.e., for a forehand bottom turn, place more weight onto the balls of your feet – especially the rear foot – and toes. This probably sounds fairly straightforward but the exact timing and amount of weight transferred from heels to toes and the balance between the front and rear feet are only acquired through trial and error. You will gradually acquire a feel for the move. Remember to keep the legs flexed and your centre of gravity low as you begin your turn.

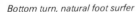

Bottom turn, natural foot surfer

Page 35 shows a natural foot doing a forehand bottom turn, and the drawing below shows two goofy-foot surfers doing bottom turns at the same time.

Trimming

Page 37 shows a goofy-foot surfer 'trimming' across the face of a small right. Trimming is the term used to describe the constant but small alterations in weight shift to allow the board to plane in the most direct route across the wave face. To the casual observer it probably looks as if the surfer isn't doing very much but in fact subtle weight changes are needed to keep the board at the right height on the wave. If you stay too low you will run out of 'juice' and if you stay too high the board will very quickly be left behind by the wave.

The transition from a bottom turn to an efficient trimming position takes quite a bit of getting used to. It is very easy to make the mistake of prolonging the bottom turn too long so that the board turns right up the wave face and exits over the crest. The secret is to transfer weight from the toes to the heels (after a forehand bottom turn) fairly quickly at just the right moment.

Just how long you can keep trimming across a wave for depends entirely on the characteristics of the wave of course. On a wave consisting of a peak and a very short shoulder you will very quickly run out of wave! In such cases a 'cut-back' will be required to stay with the wave, but more of that later. For the time being, if you can catch a wave, bottom-turn, trim and leave the wave when you want to, you are well on the way.

Stalling

If the fore and aft trim of a board is upset by placing too much weight on the rear foot, the board will tend to stall. Intentional stalling can be used as a functional manoeuvre but this was more common in the days of longboards when it was an efficient way of waiting for the wave to catch you up whilst trimming (whereas today a quick cut-back would be the norm).

I include stalling here to emphasise briefly the importance of maintaining the correct weight balance between the front and rear feet. Like all surfing skills this can only be developed through experience but you will soon discover that it is necessary and beneficial to place most of your weight on either the front or rear foot at certain times. For maximum speed whilst trimming, for instance, most of your weight should be forward whereas short-radius turns in small surf require a lot of weight on the rear foot.

Cutting-out

This page shows a natural foot 'cutting-out' (or breaking-out) from a small right. To get to the position in the illustration the surfer has transferred weight to the inside rail which has made the board turn to the right and climb up the wave. The logical time to cut-out is just before the whole wave collapses or just before a long 'section' breaks in front of you. On all but the smallest waves it is a great help to be travelling fairly fast to enable you to make the uphill journey.

Cutting-out tends not to have the finesse and attention it received in pre-leash days. With the board attached to your ankle it doesn't matter too much if you fall off or hang on until the wave breaks on your head and knocks you off. In spite of this trend, it is still desirable in my opinion to finish a ride under control whenever possible.

Rights of way and crowds

Surfing locations that are situated next to large centres of population become very crowded and in some of the world's busiest surfing grounds it is necessary to drive hundreds of miles along the coast to find uncrowded waves. In any case, beginners will find it very difficult to get waves to themselves amongst competent surfers in fairly good surf. The solution is to choose the least crowded waves available even if the quality isn't as high.

There is one fundamental 'right of way' that, when adhered to, helps to make surfing in company more civilised and generally more pleasant. It is important that beginners have an understanding of this code in order to avoid misunderstandings. It must also be realised though, that when the crowd situation gets most intense, group behaviour becomes very similar to that of animals in an overcrowded cage where domination is by the most aggressive and strongest.

The drawing below shows two different surfing situations on two separate waves (both breaking rightwards). On the top wave, surfer A has taken off, bottom-turned and is trimming across the wave *before* surfer B starts to take off in front of him. Surfer A has the right of way and surfer B is said to be 'droppping in' on him. On the lower wave the situation is not as clear cut. Here surfer B has started paddling for the wave and got to his feet before surfer A, and although surfer A is on the 'inside' (i.e. nearer the curl or peak), most would *Rights of way* agree that surfer B should have priority.

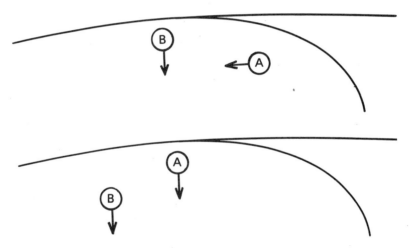

Wiping out

Something that a beginner must accept right at the start is that he will be spending quite a lot of time falling from or being knocked from his board. Even good surfers get wiped out regularly if they are pushing themselves or trying radical moves.

In small beginners' type surf the chief danger is of being tumbled around with and therefore colliding with your own board. Consequently, it is desirable to push the board away with your feet if a wipeout is inevitable. It is also a good idea to place one arm protectively across the eyes and face if there seems any chance of colliding with the board.

Chapter Four
Waves and the Weather Map

The purpose of this chapter is to give those with no knowledge of the mysteries of the weather map some idea of the possibilities and usefulness of surf prediction. For a study of the subject in much greater detail, I highly recommend a recently published book called *The Weather Surfer* by Vic Morris and Joe Nelson (Grossmont Press, San Diego).

How waves are created
A steady wind blowing across the surface of a large body of water builds waves, and the size the waves attain depends on the following factors:
  (a) Wind strength.
  (b) The length of time the wind has been blowing ('duration').
  (c) The distance of open water over which the wind has been blowing at a fairly steady speed and in a fairly constant direction ('fetch').
  (d) Water depth. Shallow water inhibits wave growth.
  Although rideable waves occur in small seas and big lakes, the best surf arrives at the edges of the major oceans where potential fetch is vast and when the wind and waves don't arrive at the same time (ideally, the wind doesn't arrive at all).
  Ocean waves that have left their turbulent source areas behind are called swells. A swell, although suffering very gradual 'decay', is capable of travelling many thousands of miles through calm, deep water. Very big swells can travel through areas of strong contrary winds and conflicting wave movement without major modification.

Isobars and surf
In order to estimate the likelihood of a swell in your area for a two to three day period, you will need to study the current weather chart covering the ocean area which produces your waves. Such charts are shown on television and are available in some daily newspapers. In

Paddlers perspective at Lunada Bay, California (Woody Woodworth)

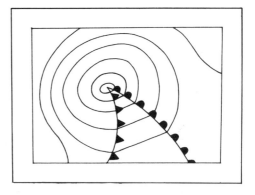

Britain, *The Guardian* gives a very good chart for that particular day whereas the chart in the *Daily Telegraph*, though useful, is of the previous day. Local winds can be estimated from these charts too, but in any case such information is easily gathered from shipping forecasts and local weather reports. In certain parts of the world, swell forecasts are broadcast as well.

Wind strength and direction are assessed from a weather chart by observation of the density and layout of the 'isobars'. An isobar is simply a line joining points of equal atmospheric pressure. If you are familiar with contour lines on large scale maps, then the principles of isobars will be fairly easy to understand. The average pressure over the oceans is 1010 millibars. The factors affecting the movement of the atmosphere and climate are varied and the interrelation between them is very complex. The three chief influences are: heat from the sun, the earth's rotation and the effects of large areas of water and land masses.

Most parts of the world, especially those away from the tropics, have seasons marked by distinct changes in weather patterns. The time of year therefore has a great influence over surf quality and personal comfort. The areas of the major oceans producing most swells are well away from the tropics and their swell-producing potential is also seasonal.

By far the most important sources of good surfing waves are the areas of low pressure and high winds called 'depressions' found in the North Atlantic, North Pacific and Southern Ocean (which includes the South Pacific). These depressions are generally deeper, cover a larger area and are more common in the winter season of the respective ocean. Summer depressions are smaller and are usually situated in higher latitudes.

The other main source of swells, though less important than depressions, is the tropical cyclone. An intense cyclone, with winds reaching more than 65 knots, is known as a hurricane. The tropical parts of the following ocean areas have specific seasons when hurricanes may occur: the South Pacific, North-east Pacific and North-west Pacific, the Indian Ocean and North-west Atlantic.

High winds exist whenever there is a marked difference in pressure in one area. This is known as a 'steep pressure gradient' and is shown on a chart by the abundance of isobars over a relatively short distance. Steep pressure gradients are almost always associated with areas of low pressure.

Areas of calm or very light winds are a feature of high pressure. Large, spherical areas of high pressure are called anti-cyclones while elongated strips of it are called ridges.

Winds always circulate around pressure systems. In the northern hemisphere, air flow is anti-clockwise around a depression, with the wind travelling roughly parallel with the isobars but at a slight angle ('indraft') towards the low centre. In northern hemisphere highs, the winds still run roughly parallel with the isobars but with a slight angle outwards towards lower pressure. When the pressure gradient in a high is very weak, other factors apart from isobar orientation affect wind direction (see section on local winds). In the southern hemisphere, features of air flow are identical except that the directions of circulation are the opposite of those in the north – clockwise around a low and anti-clockwise around a high.

The important swell-producing depressions are usually fairly mobile. Those of the North Atlantic and

Wave anatomy

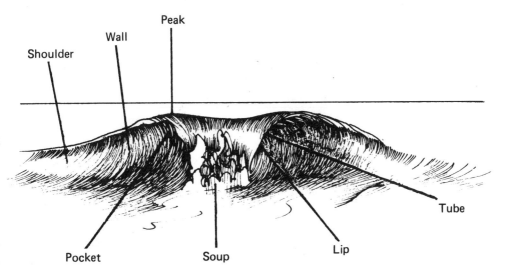

Shoulder

Wall

Peak

Pocket

Soup

Lip

Tube

North Pacific travel in a direction between east and north-east and those of the Southern Ocean move in a general easterly or south-easterly direction. The speed of their movement varies but rarely exceeds thirty knots. Partly because of this general eastward drift of depressions, land to the east of their position invariably receives much stronger swell than land to the west. Swell will also last longer if the depression is particularly slow moving.

One of the drawbacks of surfing areas in fairly high latitudes, such as Ireland and south-west Britain, is that the depression and its accompanying swell will quite often arrive at the same time bringing surf-wrecking onshore winds. In winter time, when the procession of lows across the North Atlantic reaches a peak, the swell from a low out at sea can be ruined by the presence in the surfing area of the previous low.

Page 45 shows a simplified and rather stylised weather chart of the North-east Atlantic indicating excellent surf potential for the exposed parts of Western Europe. The arrows on the chart indicate wind direction in several key areas.

Although the size and speed of any depression will affect swell potential, its shape is very important as well. Not only is the pressure gradient steepest in the southern part of the low in the illustration but the isobars there are fairly straight. The fetch in that area at any one time therefore is greater than if the isobars were more rounded. The biggest swell from this depression will arrive in the areas that are in line with the area of greatest fetch but just how big that swell will be, will also depend on the age and the movement of the depression itself.

It is important to allow sufficient time for newly-formed swells to arrive. My chart gives no clue to the history of the depression. A swell from a freshly-formed small depression centred in the same area would generally take about three days to reach south-west England.

The rather optimistic-looking anti-cyclone over Spain will provide light offshore winds on the surfing coasts of France, south-west England and Ireland so creating the perfect surfing picture!

Local winds
During summertime as well as in the warmer parts of the world in general, what are known as land and sea breezes are common whenever a large area of high pressure creates a very weak pressure gradient. They occur because the land both warms up and cools down

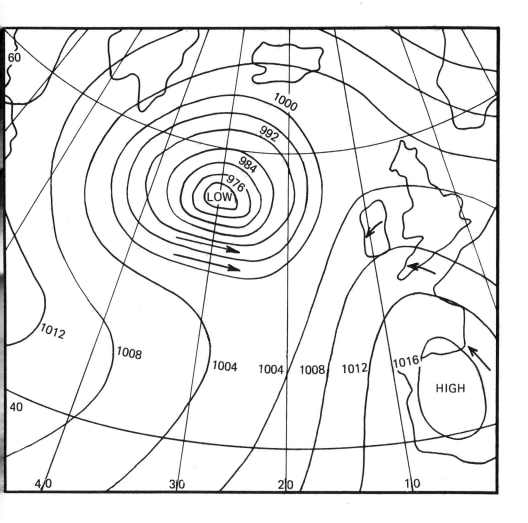

much more quickly than the ocean does. Consequently, as soon as the sun gets really hot in the morning, relatively cool air moves onshore from the sea to replace the warmer, rising air over the land. By late evening, because of rapid heat loss from the land by radiation, cool air flows seawards. In conjunction with a swell, the offshore land breeze is usually sufficient to brush the waves to perfection, whereas the sea breeze is always strong enough to ruin everything.

Because the offshore land breeze is a phenomenon of the nighttime, it is dark for most of the time it occurs. Fortunately though, it overlaps into the early morning and begins again before dark in the evening. It nearly always lasts for more of the morning daylight than of the evening, so to make the most of it, get up *early*.

45

Chapter Five
Types of Break and Where to Surf

Although the swell and wind direction discussed in Chapter 4 are of great importance from a surfer's point of view, two additional factors are equally important, namely (a) the shape of the coastline and the configuration of the seabed in the surfing area; and (b) the way in which large tides alter the position of the surf and therefore the type of seabed over which it breaks at any one time.

Beach and sandbar breaks
By far the most common type of surfing area is that provided by a normal sandy beach, with or without the addition of banks or bars. 'Beach breaks', as they are called, are the best type of break for beginners because they lack sharp projections against which the surfer can be thrown.

Since sand is such mobile material and waves are highly efficient movers of sand, you will find that the contours of a surfing beach change from day to day. Beaches that shelve very gradually produce slow-breaking and rather uninteresting waves, whereas those with the biggest humps and dips possess more scope for faster and hollower waves. On the other hand, the sandbars invariably lie parallel to the advancing wave crests so that sections of a wave will often break all at once ('sectioning'), rather than 'peeling' on arriving at breaking depth, or alternatively the waves will break across the whole surfing area or bay causing unrideable surf ('closing out').

An important exception to this general trend with sandbars is where sand has accumulated against a man-made feature such as a groyne or pier. The sand here is often a fairly permanent feature and since the edge of such a sandbank is sometimes at an angle to the wave crests, the waves thus created are well-shaped with a relatively predictable take-off position.

Reef and point breaks
When good quality reef or point breaks are readily available, the experienced surfer will rarely bother with

Lennox Head, New South Wales (Surfing World)

47

Reef break, Hawaii (Surfing World)

beach breaks in the same area. Unfortunately, neither are exactly abundant.

Because rideable reefs and points are composed of fairly permanent material such as bedrock, coral or large boulders, (or, rarely, stranded whales and wrecked ships), they are extremely reliable and predictable when compared to an ordinary sandy beach. The wave-shape is usually very good (often powerful), the take-off area remains constant (either at one particular spot or along a certain axis), and in the case of points, the rides can be very long with ample scope to string moves together and generally play around.

Traditionally, reef breaks are depicted as having waves that will break you and your board in half as soon as you go near them. I suppose this is a fairly natural attitude after the bombardment of sensational shots and photographs we get in movies and magazines. Reef breaks can, however, be quite small and very, very sweet. Many stretches of rocky coastline are worth a reappraisal. What a pleasant surprise when that insignificant looking wave just offshore turns out, on casual inspection, to be 4ft high and perfect.

The most obvious hazard with regard to surfing reefs and points, is landing at speed on the nasty material of which they are composed. Although they are obviously not good places for beginners, it is worth bearing in

Point break, Kirra Point, Queensland
(Surfing World)

mind that they are not always jagged and, in any case, wet sand is about as kind as concrete when you hit it at high velocity.

One great advantage of most reefs (and some points), is that because of the close proximity of deep water, access to the break is relatively easy as long as you don't mind a long paddle. This not only applies to the initial paddle out but to the paddle in as well, even if you do change your mind about riding on closer inspection. There is also, of course, ease of paddling back to the take-off area after each ride.

Once you've got over the initial 'psyche-out' of the rocks 'just down there', a co-operative reef or point can actually be a friendlier place to surf than an adjacent beach. This is especially true in larger surf when by the time you've got outside at the beach you've been half pounded to death and you're exhausted. Know the feeling?

One last word about rocky spots. If you are going to (or end up by having to) walk over coral, sea urchins or rock with barnacles and mussel shells, wear neoprene socks with hard soles. Skin gets very soft after saltwater immersion!

The effects of tide
As Vic Morris and Joe Nelson point out in their book *The Weather Surfer*, in areas with a big tidal range, the state of the tide is almost everything. They then go on to cite New England as an area with a 'big' range of 10ft. It may interest you boys in New England to learn that us boys in North Devon have to contend with a spring tide range of 30ft! In this neck of the woods, the tide *is* everything.

Wherever an ocean enters a long tapering inlet or a large estuary, the rise and fall of the tide is accentuated. In mid-ocean the rise and fall is minimal – that of the Hawaiian Islands, for instance, is only 2 ft.

Since a great variety of seabed is covered and uncovered so rapidly in areas with big tides, you quickly learn the need to be mobile and 'work the tides' (where chores such as school and work allow). Big tides mean that trying to predict where the next good set on a beach break is going to peak becomes a matter of guesswork and that reef showing well at low tide will be good for an hour and a half if you're very lucky.

It would be futile for me to attempt to list the types of break that work at set tides. There is no regular pattern and the larger the tides, the greater the need for accurate local knowledge and a certain amount of slick operating. Each location with a variety of breaks has a spot that shows best at low tide, another that shows best at high and yet others that work at certain times in between.

Two important points worth remembering if you're travelling and surfing beach breaks. Firstly, a beach that is steep at the high tide mark is useless around high tide. Secondly, a weak swell often shows best at low tide.

Rips

When fairly large surf is breaking on a beach, the extra volume of water that is carried shorewards during the whitewater 'surge' of each set has to escape seawards again. In order to do this, the extra water naturally picks the line of least resistance. On an open beach, this water will flow parallel to the shore along the channel inside the innermost sandbank and then head out to sea as soon as it reaches a channel that breaches the sandbank. In a small bay bordered by rocks, or at the rocky end of a larger bay, the rip will lie in the channel formed by the scouring away of sand along the edge of the rocks. In larger surf, especially when the sets are continuous, rips are usually very obvious and simulate quite powerful rivers!

From a safety point of view (which affects swimmers as much as surfers), it is essential to be aware of rips and to realise that to paddle a board or to swim against a strong rip is impossibie. The way into the beach is via the whitewater where the depth is less. If you want to get out of a rip that is moving seawards (in order to reach breaking surf and hence the beach), you will need to *steadily* make your way parallel to the beach to gain the nearest breaking waves. Assuming however, that you really do want to surf in conditions producing powerful rips, use the rip to get outside.

Always spend sufficient time assessing the size of the surf and the size and frequency of the big sets, and *then* commit yourself if you're happy. With strong rips running, the only way back in is on a wave!

Chapter Six
Surfing

But, more and more, other kids and a few grownups would stand around and watch. And, naturally, they would point out that one surfer was better than another. I was puzzled by the whole thing. But it was the ruin of me. I wanted to be the guy pointed out as the best. The seed of ego had been planted. I wasn't the best. Not by anybody's standards.

But I sure as hell wanted to be.

Phil Edwards.
'You Should Have Been Here an Hour Ago'

Spontaneity

The danger in depicting individual manoeuvres under separate headings (as I intend doing in this chapter), is that a beginner may presume that they are thought of and performed in isolation from other moves by a surfer of average ability. In reality, of course, a reasonable wave will be ridden by a competent surfer in a very fluid manner where all the recognisable moves merge together. As will be realised, it is the precise nature of the wave that dictates the kinds of moves that can be (or must be) utilised. It would be rather futile, for instance, to go out with the intention of practising one particular manoeuvre if the waves just won't allow it.

As a developing surfer gradually progresses and masters a sufficient repertoire of skills to be fairly mobile, his reaction to a given situation on a wave becomes more and more spontaneous. He won't for instance think like this: 'Now then, this wave seems to be very weak, I'm right out on the shoulder and unless I do something quick I'm going to run out of wave completely; okay a cutback, now then, step back with the rear foot and. ...' He will have done a cutback *before* getting bogged down way out on the shoulder and without even thinking about it.

As well as being able to throw your board around a bit, it is necessary to be able to anticipate roughly what the wave is going to do in the near future and to be able to assess your own likely position on the wave in two or three seconds time. Experience is the only way in which these skills will be acquired.

Kneeboarder in action (Surfing World)

Reading a wave and wave knowledge
Being able to predict roughly what a breaking wave is going to do is part of the art of 'reading' a wave. By being in and around surf for long periods over a number of years, you will gradually acquire a high level of what is often referred to as 'wave knowledge'. This simply means the ability to assess an individual wave or a surf situation accurately. The best surfers have an uncanny way (a sixth sense almost) of knowing which wave to catch, which wave not to catch, which part of the wave to catch, and exactly when to cut out a split second before the wave jumps on their head.

Style
Each surfer develops a style of his own, even though he may not be particularly aware of it himself and even though he hasn't consciously set out to develop a particular style. It is purely a matter of taste as to which styles are good to watch and which styles are not. The only thing that really matters I guess is whether a surfer's style is functional and allows him to go where he wants and whether he personally enjoys surfing that way. Narrow stance, wide stance, arm waving, body rotation, crouching, arm dragging, smoothness, or arrogance are but a few of the hallmarks that may individually contribute to one person's style.

In the last few years, skateboarding has had a very marked effect on certain people's surfing style (especially shortboard riding on small waves), and it is said that skiing can have an influence too.

More on catching waves
In all but the highest levels of the sport, surfers frequently experience difficulty in catching waves for one reason or another. It hardly needs me to point out that unless you go out and catch plenty of waves, you're not going to have much of a surfing session. Because of the absolutely fundamental necessity of catching waves therefore, it may be useful to take a closer look at the requirements.

Without wave-catching ability being the number one priority when choosing your board, it must be remembered that board design can make a lot of difference. Slightly longer and more buoyant boards can be paddled faster, and wider boards (especially in the tail area) will plane earlier and more easily on small waves.

Any surfboard, especially a present day shortboard, requires a steep enough wave on which to start planing. In view of this fact, your position in relation to where the waves are steep enough (just before they break) is critical. While surfing a beach break you will need to be constantly on the move. The bigger the tides, the more mobile you will have to become. A good ploy in crowded conditions is to ride the smaller inside waves and leave the masses to wait for, and fight over, the larger set waves further out.

When the surf gets big, different sets of factors come into play – most of them psychological. The chief problem is whether you *really* want to catch the waves in the first place! Often when the surf is bigger than normal at a particular spot, you see only about a quarter of the guys out actually riding anything. When the surf gets bigger than you're accustomed to riding, aggressive desire is by far the most important aid to catching waves! It is very easy in these conditions to paddle like a madman for the horizon when an extra big set looms up and then stay much too far outside after it's gone through. In the meantime, the smaller sets that you'd be willing to catch are peaking about a hundred yards inside. Inevitably, you've just paddled in again to catch some of the more reasonable waves when the next big one arrives and you get absolutely hammered. It's one of the most efficient ways of experiencing extreme fear and intense frustration at the same time.

When a strong offshore wind is blowing, the difficulties of wave catching become intensified. Bearing in mind that the waves will break a bit later than they would without the offshore wind, it is usually necessary to position yourself a little further inside. If you attempt to stand up too soon in these conditions, you are either

Fading take-off

blown back off the wave or you get locked in the lip and go 'over the falls'. Going over the falls can be very exhilarating but should be avoided if possible. So, to prevent disappointments it is a good idea to take one or two more paddle strokes to take you *down* the wave face slightly before attempting to stand up. A board with a fairly narrow nose (hence less wind resistance), helps matters considerably.

Pages 55 and 56 show two important alternatives to a normal straight take-off. Page 55 shows a 'fading' takeoff where, although the surfer intends riding the wave towards his right, he is fading to his left in order to get closer to the peak before doing his first bottom turn. His precise position in the drawing is very similar to the latter stages of a cutback. Page 56 shows an 'angled' takeoff in a backhand direction. The surfer depicted here has decided that the wave is so steep and close to breaking at the takeoff spot that he wouldn't have sufficient time to make the drop and bottom turn successfully if he used a conventional straight takeoff. If a wave is sufficiently steep and juicy for an angled takeoff to be feasible, it is a very quick way of making the transition from takeoff to fast, efficient tracking. If the waves are super-fast and hollow on the other hand, the only option is to drop straight down the face and make a very carefully timed turn at the bottom.

Angled take-off

Positioning

Largely as a result of the ultra-manoeuvrability of the modern shortboard, it is the general aim these days to stay as close to the peak or curl of a wave as possible. Not only is this the steepest and most powerful part of the wave that is rideable but it is here that the finest degree of judgement is necessary and it is the domain that offers the most intense experiences and visual effects. In a relatively small number of surf spots the waves are capable of 'tubing' with room inside the tube for surfer plus board. On such occasions, even though the waves may be quite small, the most intense and sought after surfing experience is to 'get tubed', and preferably, but rarely, to disappear from sight completely and then reappear still in control. Since the vast majority of ridden waves definitely don't tube, the best you can aim for is to stay close to where the wave is breaking and hence retain the speed and manoeuvrability that the steepest un-broken part of the wave is able to provide.

The purpose of all functional surfing moves (even though they may be exhilarating in their own right) is to allow you to maintain a good position on a wave for as long as possible. Some moves, such as 'stalling' or 'climbing and dropping' are used as delaying tactics to allow the juicy part of the wave to catch you up, whilst something like a cut-back is a very definite return to the source of power.

Trimming for speed

As was implied in chapter 3, there is far more skill involved in efficient trimming than may be obvious through casual observation. When a wave is breaking very quickly, you will need to travel fast across the face to 'make' the wave or a particular section. In circumstances like this, a fairly direct route at the right height will be the only answer. Deviations from the straight line will have to wait until you're out on the shoulder and the wave has slowed down.

Sometimes a surfer will trim fairly high across the face of a meaty looking wave. If he attempts to track higher up, the face would be too steep and he would 'spin-out', but if he went lower he would lose most of the power and speed that gravity is able to provide in his present position. For maximum speed whilst trimming, most of your weight should be forward over the front foot. This is especially true of boards with lots of tail lift because at speed such boards will automatically lift at the nose and cause the planing efficiency to be hindered.

Opposite. *Climbing and dropping*

Climbing and dropping

The easiest way to slow your speed down so that the more interesting part of a good wave can catch you up is to climb and drop. This is the term used to describe a series of linked S-turns executed while travelling in the same direction. By engaging and disengaging the inside rail the surfer makes his board alternately climb up and then drop down the wave face.

The sequence of illustrations on page 58 shows a surfer starting off a series of climb and drop moves.

Off the lip

On this page a surfer is shown performing an 'off the lip' on a small wave. Such a manoeuvre is the logical extension of the climb part of climbing and dropping, where the surfer has gone as high as possible without accidentally cutting out. The normal sequel to this move is an 'off the bottom' (an abbreviated bottom turn), which may lead, slingshot fashion, into another off the lip, and so on.

Notice in the drawing the way in which the legs have been bent as the board hits the lip. They will then be extended slightly as the board drops down the face again. The legs are constantly being used as shock absorbers to iron out bumps and to compensate for sudden changes in direction. The skiing terms 'weighting' and 'un-weighting' are just as valid and important in surfing.

Off the lip

Opposite. *A cutback leading into a forehand turn*

The cut-back

Few moves in surfing are as satisfying as a well-executed, high-speed, flowing cut-back, especially when used functionally as an efficient and very quick return to the juice. This is even truer if the cut-back is performed in a backhand direction. Page 62 shows two variations of a natural-foot doing a backhand cut-back. It is essential that a cut-back is started from *high* on the wave. This allows sufficient time and maintenance of speed for a full 180-degree turn to be completed while moving down the wave face.

I have avoided so far saying anything about moving your feet about on the board's deck. This needs to be done much less on small modern equipment than in the old days. There are times however, when quick, small steps are necessary and the preparation just before a cut-back is such a time. Just before you commence the sweeping turn from high on the wave, take a step back with the rear foot and transfer extra weight onto it. This will briefly reduce the turning arc of your board and get you on the way. The only time this may not be necessary is when a very short board is being used in conjunction with an extra-wide stance.

For a cut-back to be possible in the first place, the wave must be sufficiently large and you must be going fast enough *initially* to maintain planing speed through such a long turn.

Cutback (Surfing World)

Cutback

Cutback

The re-entry

A functional re-entry is the kind of manoeuvre that can
be used to get past a short collapsing section of wave.
The idea with a re-entry is to go very high on the wave
with sufficient speed to carry you *over* the collapsing
part in order to re-enter green water just beyond it. The
breaking section has to be quite small for this move to
be successful. The most difficult part of a re-entry is the
transition from the floating, weightless part where the
board is riding over more air than water, to the sudden
engagement of the inside rail on the far side.

A re-entry is often used as a last ditch, nothing-to-
lose, attempt to get one last bit of fun out of a wave
that is about to close-out. In such cases, the re-entry is
closely followed by the all too familiar problem of what
to do with a continuous line of soup (if you stay on your
feet that is). The sequence on page 64 shows a
functional re-entry.

A more difficult variation on the above theme is where
the surfer makes a 180-degree turn in the soup and then
re-enters in the direction he came *from*. This is known as
a 'rebound'.

Nose-riding

In the days of big boards, people used to become
obsessed with posing right at the front of the board. For
a while there were even nose riding competitions.
Forever after, 'hanging-five' and 'hanging-ten' were to
be automatically linked with surfing by the non-surfing
public!

The old fashioned style of nose-riding was
undoubtedly a skilled business but it was made possible
in the first place by the sheer length and area of the long
boards and was aided even further by increased tail lift.
These days, nose-riding is most likely to be used as an
extreme form of weight-forward trimming for maximum
speed. Only at high speed will a position very close to
the nose be able to be maintained for any length of time.

Tube riding

Pages 65 and 66 both show surfers tubed in different sized waves. Page 63 illustrates a surfer who is really only partially tubed in a small wave. He is having to crouch very low on the board in order to fit into the very confined space that the wave is able to offer. On page 66 the wave is larger and the tube is more spacious. The surfer in this drawing (who is viewed from further along the wave), is completely inside the tube and is able to maintain a more upright stance. Viewed from the beach, the surfer would be completely hidden by the falling lip.

Breaking waves which tube in a cooperative and rideable fashion are extremely rare. The necessary ingredients are a powerful, clean swell being forced to break by a very sudden decrease in depth and where the breaking depth contour is at a slightly oblique angle to the wave crest.

Even though it may be feasible to get inside a tubing wave, it is a different matter entirely to get out again. Note the thickness of the lip ahead of the surfer on page 66.

Partially tubed in small wave

Opposite. *Re-entry*

Stalling

The four-drawing sequence on page 67 shows the way in which a stall can be used to slow down progress sufficiently to get tubed on a suitable wave.

In drawing number one, the surfer has taken off and is part way through a bottom turn. The lip near his original take off position is just starting to form a small tube. In drawing two, the tube is growing and is becoming better formed. The surfer here has transferred a lot of weight to his rear foot and has started to stall the board. Drawing three shows him part way through the stall. The tube has nearly caught him up and, all being well, he is about to get 'covered up'. The last drawing in the sequence shows the surfer in the position he was hoping to attain. He is now tubed and has moved his weight forward to regain maximum speed.

When both the waves and the surfers are sufficiently good, a 'tube stall' (i.e. a stall *inside* the tube) can be used either to prolong the time inside or to get more deeply tubed.

Opposite. Stalling to become tubed

Kneeboarding

The art of kneeboarding is really a separate bag of tricks from stand up surfing, even though they both have much in common. It is extremely popular in Australia and seems to be gradually gaining more interest around the world. Modern kneeboards are just as long as the smallest standup boards (i.e. 5ft 9in—6ft), and are generally very wide (24—25in). Page 69 shows a typical planshape.

Even though the idea of using a kneeboard is very appealing, I have still to give it a try. As it is, even though it looks and sounds great, I must limit my comments to the most obvious points. These have been arrived at purely through observation and from the enthusiastic ravings of kneeboarding mates.

One of the most important facts about kneeboarding is the pure ability, because of compactness, to fit into very small or narrow tubes — places that would be virtually unattainable on a standup board.

Due no doubt to the mechanical advantage gained from swim fins, paddling is less strenuous and therefore less hassle. Owing to a kneeboard's shortness and the very low riding position, they are both ultra-manoeuvrable and extremely stable. There is no such

Lynne Boyer at Sunset Beach (Island Style)

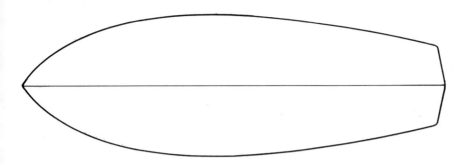

Kneeboard

thing as 'forehand' and 'backhand', and the closeness
of the surfer's face to the water surface results in a
more immediate and apparently more interesting visual
experience.

Because it is easier and quicker to get to your knees
than it is to get to your feet, a kneeboarder is able to
catch a wave generally much later than the others. It is a
fairly common sight to see a knee-rider freefall down
part of the face and recover with apparent ease. They
are able therefore, to sit 'inside' the bulk of stand-
uppers and catch a lot of waves.

Now the bad news. Because the shock-absorbing
effect of the legs is restricted, the body tends to be
bounced around quite a lot. (A large neoprene deck
patch, in place of wax, softens the jolting a bit.) A
kneeboard doesn't take kindly to excess surface chop.
More gear is necessary because, besides fins, you really
need mini-leashes to attach each fin to the ankle and
when the water is cold, very thin neoprene socks need
to be worn inside the fins. From a spectator's point of
view, the kneelers certainly look less elegant than those
standing up, though this has very little to do with the
enjoyment of the participants.

Chapter Seven
Further Board Design

Because of the practice and tradition of custom board construction, surfing has offered perfectly the opportunity for 'one-off' experimentation. Due to this fact, shapers are able to change design features one at a time, if they so wish, so that the validity of that particular alteration can be more fairly assessed. However, because the style and handling preferences of each surfer are unique and because the vast majority of custom boards are required to cope with at least a limited range of conditions, different sets of design features are blended together in an endless variety of ways. Consequently, the whole area of design is complex and because it bristles with so many apparent contradictions, it can be very confusing.

In order that a relative newcomer to surfing can order a custom board with some degree of confidence, I have attempted in this chapter to cover all the major design variables whose *effects* seem to be widely accepted. To be fairly comprehensive there are planshapes and descriptions of some types of boards that have been designed for very specific types of surf and they are therefore, rather extreme. Perhaps the most important thing to remember when thinking in terms of a new board is the fact that if you only intend to own one board and hope to surf in a reasonable range of wave types, any of the 'extreme' types of board will be severely limiting.

Loading, area and planshape
The characteristics of airflow around the wings of birds and aeroplanes are very similar to those of water flow around a surfboard. The term 'wing loading' is used to describe the total weight of, let's say, a particular type of bird in relation to its total wing area. For example, the wing loading of a Barn Owl is 3.4sq. cm per gram, while that of a Peregrine Falcon is 1.1sq. cm. The 'wing' loading of a surfboard could also be calculated by relating the area of the board's bottom with the total

McCoy winger swallow-tail (Surfing World)

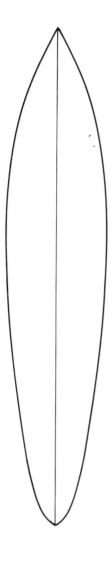

weight of board plus surfer. The *actual* physical loading or water pressure acting on the bottom of a board will depend upon its position at any one time. Greatest pressure will be encountered during a bottom turn after dropping down the face of a big wave, whereas zero pressure could be experienced during an 'off the top' or an 'off the lip'. The most important thing to remember from a design point of view is the effect of your own body weight in relation to the board's area, hence the different sizes of board recommended for beginners in chapter one.

Let's imagine two competent surfers, one lighter than average and the other heavier than average, riding identical boards of 'moderate' all-round design in 6ft surf. The light surfer's board will start to plane earlier during takeoff but the other guy will get more speed from the drop and will be able to travel faster while trimming. If the waves are backing off, the heavy surfer will stop planing at a higher speed than the other one. The heavy surfer will also have to be travelling relatively faster to be able to cut back as far as the light one and so on. Probably the most common mistake is that of fairly heavy surfers attempting to ride smallish waves on boards with insufficient width (especially at the tail).

As long as there is sufficient power, sailing craft and power boats fitted with foils can travel at incredibly high speeds when foil-borne. This is because the foils on which the craft are planing have a very small 'wetted area'. With enough motive power, the ultimate speed which any planing craft will attain is directly governed by wetted area simply by the amount of drag it causes. In fact, at planing speeds, wetted area is much more important than at sub-planing speeds when a craft is floating normally and is supported by straightforward displacement (waterline *length* then becomes a critical factor for instance).

A very narrow surfboard, say 16in maximum width, will travel at extremely high speeds on a big clean wave *in a straight line*. Since we must consider functions such as paddling out, wave catching and turning however, a board of this narrowness is not practical. The design of even the most extreme big-wave boards has to be the result of practical compromise.

Stated in very broad terms, big-wave boards are long and narrow, small-wave boards are short and wide and boards for 'in between' waves range between the two. Big waves require stable boards that are capable of drawing the long-drawn-out turns that are necessary at high speed, whereas small waves require early planers that are quick to turn.

Fast, streamlined boards for big-wave riding have always been known as 'guns'. The most extreme versions of these, which can be as long as 10ft, are sometimes called 'big guns' or 'rhino chasers'. Even though the term 'shortboard' is a misnomer for such surfboards, their length is the only thing they have in common with the old fashioned 'longboards'. The 7ft 10in by 19$\frac{1}{2}$in pintail on page 72 is also a big-wave board and in fact would be quite adequate for the biggest waves that most of us would be prepared to tackle. (It takes a rare blend of boldness and fanaticism to venture regularly into waves over twelve feet.)

The 6ft 10in by 20$\frac{1}{2}$in round pin winger below left is an example of a typical 'middle of the road' board capable of handling quite a large range of surf size (say from about 4ft to 8ft), without being radical or extreme in any way. For somebody who's fairly heavy, or simply wants more paddling speed, the 7ft 2in round pintail below right would be a functional alternative.

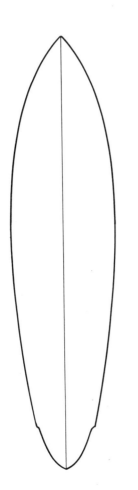

In the last ten years or so many different types of short board have been designed specially for small waves. Even though possibilities for minor design and dimension alterations are limitless, three main types have been widely accepted. These are, in chronological order, the 'fish' from California, and the 'stinger' and 'twin-fin' from Hawaii.

The fish owes its origin to a Californian kneeboarder called Steve Lis. Lis' original double pintail boards were about 5ft long and were designed just for knee-riding. It was gradually realised that the fish, with its amazing planing speed on tiny waves and high degree of manoeuvrability, would perhaps be a good stand up surfboard if made longer. The drawing on the left shows the kind of fish planshape that became very popular for 'conventional' standup surfing in the late 60s and early 70s.

It has always been realised that wide-tail (i.e. small wave) surfboards would spin out easily if fitted with a conventional, centre-placed fin. The alternatives consist

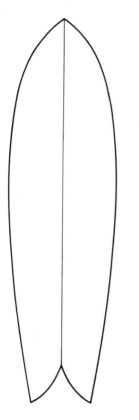

Fish

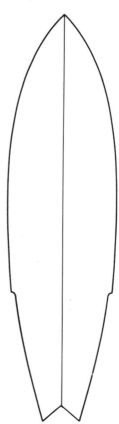

Stinger

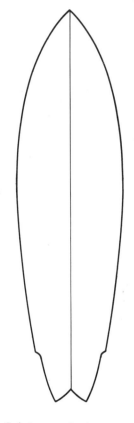

Twin fin (winger swallow)

of either a deeper single fin, or two small fins, one near each rail. Steve Lis and other early fish builders chose the latter approach and placed their fins one on each side and parallel to each other. In 1971 a famous competition surfer called David Nuuhiwa shaped himself a fish and made a lasting contribution to the ideas about functional fin placement by pointing the leading edges of the fin bases towards the nose ('toed in'), and splaying the tips outwards. This type of twin-fin setting has been widely accepted and is still currently used on modern twin-fin shapes. It takes a great deal of trust (and probably a Ph.D. in hydrodynamics), to take in all the rather esoteric justifications for this rather strange looking fin set-up but it certainly seems to make the boards looser. Purpose built jigs are used for accurate placement of the fins and although specific dimensions vary with board size, a fairly typical set-up would be: front of bases $10^1/_2$in apart, rear of bases $11^1/_2$in apart, and tips $12^1/_2$in apart.

Longer (up to 7ft 3in) and narrower fish have been designed for larger waves. Such boards, dubbed 'rocket-fish', some with single fins, seem to have met with only a varying degree of success.

In the mid-70s, one of the most highly respected board designers in Hawaii, Ben Aipa, built a board he called the 'Sting'. Aipa intended his boards, which became more popularly known as 'stingers', to be built in a whole range of lengths and widths and to therefore work in a wide range of conditions. As things turned out however, the most popular stingers have been the shorter, wider ones which are most suitable for small waves. Page 74 shows the typical planshape of such a board. In the March 1975 issue of *Surfer* magazine, Aipa said of the original design: 'The sting is actually two boards in one: the front is a small-wave board (meaning something with more width) and the other third is a more racy or speed-line shape.' In the bottom of Aipa's early stingers there was a small step or bevel running between the two wings. Board builders didn't bother with these after a while, partly because they didn't seem to make much difference but mainly because they were difficult to glass! Stingers are weight-forward, front-foot surfboards; in other words, a short radius, pivot turn is most easily accomplished with a lot more weight on the front foot than normal. This takes some getting used to and also makes the transition back to a more 'normal' board (for bigger surf for instance) quite difficult.

At the time of writing, the most popular small-wave board is the twin-fin design, left, made popular via the media, by an Australian surfing phenomenon called Mark Richards. After seeing Reno Abellira ride a 5ft 7in twin-fin at the 1976 'Coke Contest' in 2ft mush, Mark Richards has since commented: 'I was looking for a board to surf in 2–3ft waves that I could rip on and not have the tail sink after each turn. The twin-fin was the perfect solution with its tail area.' (*Surfer*, July 1978). One of the most notable things about an M. R. twin-fin is the fact that the width 1ft from the tail is wider (up to 2in) than the width 1ft from the nose. The two fins are toed-in and splayed at the tips (similar to a fish), and usually the *inner* surface of each fin is dead flat and the outer surfaces are foiled in the normal way (i.e. each fin is asymmetrical). Twin-fin section and planshapes are illustrated on page 78.

Tail variations

Page 74 shows nine of the most popular tail planshapes. Variations in size and detail based on the main themes shown are limitless.

Surfboards with wings are often called 'flyers' in Australia. Wings are sometimes claimed to have several different functions, but whether these claims are valid seems to be a matter of opinion. Their chief purpose in my view is to maintain sufficient width in the planing area (the area under the back foot) but to *reduce wetted area* in the tail region. The tail section is largely an area of water *release* and so a carefully applied reduction in area can give more speed.

Tail plan shapes

The function of a swallow tail is similar to that of wings except that the reduction in wetted area is right at the back and a straighter rail can be maintained if required (e.g. the fish).

Because different types of tail planshape are very distinctive and because they create a very convenient method of labelling different boards, their importance is usually overestimated when compared with other factors. They are also easy to depict in two dimensions, whereas certain other design features need to be seen in three dimensions to be fully appreciated.

Tail plans, when considered purely in their own right, are less important than rocker, lateral bottom shape, thickness distribution, overall planshape and rail section.

Rail shape and section

The planshape or curvature of a board's rails is to a large extent dictated by the board's overall length and width. A long, narrow pintail will have straighter rails than a short, wide pintail for instance. In all types of modern boards, the rail describes a very smooth transition from nose to tail without any pronounced 'hips'. In the cases of stingers and wingers, this smooth flow is interrupted by a small notch but in effect a whole section of rail has simply been removed; it is important to note that the rail just behind the wing is nearly always parallel to the rail just in front of it.

Rail curvature at the back of a board is dictated by width in the planing area and width at the tail – pintails allow for more curve than swallowtails for instance. People often say that more rail curve makes a board looser but if the extra curve is a result of increased width, then the ability to plane at slower speed may be more relevant than the rail shape. Curved rails aren't going to be much help at semi-planing speeds. A fish has very straight rails at the back for instance but nobody could accuse the fish design of being stiff.

The cross-section of rails is of great importance. The drawings (left) show a '50/50' rail which used to be popular in longboard days, as well as the four more efficient types of section that are used today. 'Full' rails give more buoyancy but less bite whereas the tapered rails produce the opposite effect. To a certain extent the exact hardness of rails depends on personal preference – some like them harder, some softer, but on a typical 'middle of the road' board the rails would be low throughout – starting fairly hard in the nose, becoming softer and more forgiving in the middle and then becoming increasingly hard in the tail. Ironically, it is boards intended for tiny waves on the one hand and

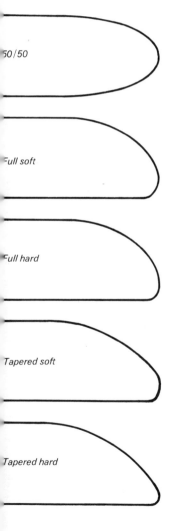

50/50

Full soft

Full hard

Tapered soft

Tapered hard

77

boards designed for tube riding on the other that require the hardest rails. When discussing his own boards for riding the celebrated 'Pipeline' in Hawaii, Gerry Lopez had the following to say: 'Edges are very hard, as oftentimes this will be the only part of the board besides the fin that is in the water. The idea is to keep the minimum amount of board in the water (for speed), with the minimum amount of effort, and still maintain some semblance of control.' (*Surfer*, May 1976).

At the other end of the wave spectrum, tiny waves are best ridden with hard-railed boards also. Hard rails will not only bite into the small amount of available face but they also contribute a great deal to sheer planing efficiency which is so vital in waves suffering from power failure.

The fin

'Besides the US car industry in the 1950s, surfers went crazy with fins in the early 70s, two's and three's were common. Me, I like one kind. A basic wide base pivot fin for vertical climbs and quick off the tail direction changes.' Terry Fitzgerald, *Sea Notes*, January 1978.

The fin provides directional stability and is an essential part of the surfboard. The most important feature of modern fins is the fact that they are 'foiled' and therefore provide 'lift' in a similar way to aeroplane wings and modern sails.

The most popular type of fin is the one designed by Dick Brewer and illustrated lower left. The dimensions of this fin are: depth – $7^5/_8$in, base length – $5^7/_8$in, thickness at base $^{15}/_{16}$ and thickness at tip $^1/_4$in.

Fin position is very much a matter of taste, but normally the tip does not project beyond the tail. Less height or base length and less foil thickness will all tend to make a board looser. Narrow-tailed boards can afford to have their fin placed further forward whereas wider-tailed boards tend to spin out rather easily unless the fin is placed well back. Fin boxes, which are very popular, allow fin position and fin type to be changed and also make transportation much safer.

Rocker and bottom shape

The kind of thickness distribution and rocker described in chapter one are typical of modern boards, although rocker requirements are slightly different for the various classes of board.

Small-wave boards need less rocker (especially tail lift) than other types to enable them to accelerate quickly and plane as fast as possible. Boards designed for larger, more powerful waves need more nose lift for

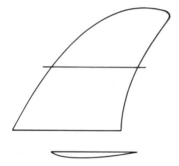

Typical fin used on Fish and Twin fins, with cross section

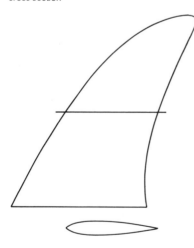

Typical fin used on single fin boards, with cross section

steep takeoffs and extra tail lift (behind the fin) to loosen them up. The exception to this general rule is boards designed for straight-line surfing on big, hollow waves which often have only limited tail lift which, in a similar way to little boards, makes for swift acceleration and high speeds.

Bottom design is the most esoteric and confusing area of all. The front two-thirds of most surfboard bottoms are flat across but when we move towards the tail we often find a certain amount of V or even shallow concave hollows. A typical setup, which originated on speedboards but has crept into other groups, is V placed in front of the fin (to loosen up an otherwise stiff shape and to aid rail to rail exchange), with flatness behind the fin in conjunction with increased tail lift.

A typical twin-fin bottom arrangement is twin concaves between and behind the fins. Concaves have the effect of reducing rocker in the bottom while maintaining it in the rails.

Conclusion

Somebody once said that designing the perfect yacht would always be impossible because such a vessel would need to be long and short, deep and shallow, and wide and narrow all at the same time. Surfboard designers are undoubtedly faced with the same kind of task.

The answer for the surfer is to choose a functional compromise that works for you. To be able to surf well in a wide range of conditions definitely requires a variety of boards and this not only means the money to buy them but also the surfing time to be able to adapt easily from one board to another.

Chapter Eight
Safety

Although I have attempted in the previous chapters to point out the most important hazards encountered when surfing, I have also tried not to overburden the reader with all the things that *could* happen. Surfing, like any other adventurous activity, involves putting oneself at risk at certain times but while the degree of risk lessens with experience and good judgement, it increases as soon as the participant feels the need to prove something to himself or to his friends regardless. Life itself is an adventure and, for my money, it would be a pretty dull existence if one didn't take up the challenge offered by the opportunities to take part in some kind of exhilarating outdoor sport.

Any kind of sporting accident is unfortunate but the saddest ones are those that result from sheer ignorance. The aim of this chapter is to make you aware of the circumstances that could lead to an 'incident', with the hope that 'learning by experience' can be restricted to handling your own surfboard without hurting other people.

It is probably obvious to anyone who's given it much thought that a surfer needs to be 'happy' in the water. Except when confined to the smallest waves, a surfer should be a competent swimmer, though there are degrees of competence. The very first experience of being in surf from an ocean swell comes as a shock to those accustomed to swimming only in pools or off sheltered beaches. It soon becomes apparent that the waves take control of the situation, until that is, you can grasp a few fundamental skills – such as going under *before* four feet of breaking wave lands on your head. It will also become clear that travelling a certain distance through surf is much more demanding than swimming the same distance through calm water. The only way to become proficient at wading and swimming through surf is to do it in the beginning whether you have a surfboard with you or not. You can learn a lot about the nature of breaking waves and how to conserve energy

Bad tempers and battered boards are often an outcome of conditions this crowded (Island Style)

simply by playing around in the surf without a board, or by belly-boarding or bodysurfing.

The various ways in which leashes have affected surfing were discussed in chapter two. From a beginner's point of view, their most serious disadvantage is that someone who boardsurfs from the outset with a leash most likely misses out on a lot of surf swimming experience. This may not matter too much until, sooner or later, either the leash breaks or its attachment to the deck comes adrift. When this happens, and it usually occurs in heavier surf, the surfer is confronted with the task of swimming back to the shore to retrieve the board and if he has always relied on his board for transport this could well be a daunting prospect. This is one occasion when at least some experience of body surfing is very handy because the easiest way to return to the shore is by *using* the waves as much as possible. At the same time of course, it is desirable not to be pounded around too much by waves breaking right on top of you. The best trick is to submerge deep enough to avoid the main turbulence but to surface in time to utilise at least some of the shoreward-moving soup.

Even though fitness and stamina are desirable qualities for the long journey back to the beach through the surf, it would be a mistake to believe that a high swimming speed plays an important part. Awareness of the situation (which means frequently looking behind you) and surf *technique* are much more important than competition-style front crawl. In fact steady, energy-saving treading of water or using the breaststroke are the best ploys while waiting for waves, with a few quick strokes of head-down front crawl reserved for actually catching the waves you want. If you find yourself in a powerful rip, *never* try to swim against it; instead head diagonally across the rip until you can use normal breaking waves away from the influence of the rip. Above all, conserve energy and aim to arrive at the shore with strength to spare.

While constant use of a leash right from the start will perhaps prevent a beginner from gaining swimming experience in surf, I would not normally advocate surfing without one. Besides the pure convenience of having an instant-return board, a leash protects other people from your board; this not only includes other surfers but, more importantly, swimmers and paddlers nearer the beach. A fairly common sight in the holiday season is a novice's board without a leash (perhaps a big, heavy, hire board) ploughing its way towards the crowded shallows. Such a situation usually arises from ignorance

on the part of the novice surfer but this doesn't make
the impact any the less painful. Children often try to
catch loose boards as they skitter shorewards, which
makes matters worse.

Beaches with lifeguards usually have a marked
swimming area. This is not only to protect swimmers
from rips and rocks but also serves to keep missiles
such as loose boards and abandoned kayaks away from
the swimmers. Wherever beaches aren't as highly
organised as this (and sometimes when they are) surfers
inevitably end up offshore in line with other sea users. It
is only fair at such times to make sure that you are using
a leash. If you *have* to surf without a leash, find a spot
away from everybody else.

One of the most important things to avoid during a
wipeout is colliding with or being tumbled around with
your own board. If you haven't been able to get away
from your board, then its a good idea to cover your head
with your arms for protection. Ironically, most mishaps
involving collisions with the bottom occur in very small
waves breaking in shallow water. If when wiping out in
such a situation you fall shorewards, it is not a good idea
to stick one arm out rigidly in an attempt to soften the

blow. In shallow water always try to fall as flat as possible — it doesn't matter if if looks ungainly. The aim should be to present as large a body area to the water surface as possible.

After a wipeout in small surf, never be in too much of a hurry to surface again. Sometimes your board will shoot up in the air and your head will be there to receive it just when it comes down again. In earlier days when boards were much heavier, you could quite easily hear the thump of the board when it landed back on the water. The noise isn't quite as noticeable with more modern boards but it is still a good idea to put one arm over your head as you come up. Strong offshore winds are capable of flipping a light board end over end if you have just fallen off; so beware of your board being lifted *back* over the wave in these conditions.

The best advice I can give to a beginner regarding crowded surfing conditions is to avoid them altogether if possible. When the surfing gets very crowded and people start to 'drop in' on each other collisions occur and people get hurt. Whether you have to surf in crowds or not, make sure you have a full understanding of rights of way and if, as a beginner, you want to avoid trouble with other surfers, don't drop in on other people!

Glossary

BACKING OFF	When waves suddenly flatten as they move over deeper waters, e.g. a channel between sandbars.
BACKWASH	The disruptive effects of seaward moving waves, caused by wave reflection from a steep shoreline.
BOWL	A part of a surfing wave that forms a crescent shape if viewed from above.
CLEAN-UP	A pre-leash term describing a wave or a set that breaks outside of a group of surfers causing them to lose their boards.
CLOSED OUT	When waves break right across a bay or surfing area causing unrideable surf.
CRITICAL	A very steep and fast breaking portion of wave that is difficult to ride.
CUTOUT	Leaving a wave by turning up the face and over the crest.
DING	Damage to a surfboard.
DOWN THE MINE	Australian term for a wipeout.
FADE	To ride towards the breaking part of a wave.
GLASS-OFF	When the wind dies, (usually in the evening), to allow the wave surfaces to be very smooth or glassy.
GROUND SWELL	See SWELL.
GUN	A long board designed for riding big waves.
HIGHWAY SURFER	A 'poser' whose surfboard stays on the roofrack.

INSIDE	On the shoreward side of the normal breaking point of the waves.
KICK-OUT	See CUTOUT.
LINE-UP	The point where the waves are consistently starting to break.
OUTSIDE	On the seaward side of the normal breaking point of the waves.
OVER THE FALLS	To freefall with the breaking lip of a hollow wave.
PEARLING	When the nose of the board digs under the surface while being ridden.
PEELING	The way good surfing waves break, i.e. predictably and along their length.
PIG	A surfboard with its widest point behind centre.
PULLOUT	See CUTOUT.
SECTIONING	When a portion of wave breaks all at once, rather than peeling.
SET	A group of waves.
SOUP	Whitewater.
SWELL	Ocean waves no longer under the influence of the wind that created them.
SWITCHFOOT	Changing from goofy to natural foot or vice versa while riding a wave.
TAKE-OFF	Catching an unbroken wave and standing up.
WIND LIFT	The strong updraught caused by an offshore wind blowing up the face of a wave.
WIND SWELL	Surfers' term for a swell, created by a local wind, that hasn't had time to become neat and tidy.
WIPEOUT	Falling off the board or being knocked from the board by a breaking wave.